EVERYBODY DIES

Everybody Dies

A Children's Book

for Grown-Ups

by Ken Tanaka

with David Ury

HARPER DESIGN
An Imprint of HarperCollins Publishers

A Maximum Pleasant Book

EVERYBODY DIES: A CHILDREN'S BOOK FOR GROWN-UPS

HarperCollins books may be purchased for educational, business, or sales promotional use. For information, please e-mail the Special Markets Department at SPsales@harpercollins.com.

Published in 2014 by:
Harper Design
An Imprint of HarperCollins Publishers
10 East 53rd Street
New York, NY 10022
Tel (212) 207-7000
harperdesign@harpercollins.com
www.harpercollins.com

Distributed throughout the world by:
HarperCollins Publishers
10 East 53rd Street
New York, NY 10022
Library of Congress Control Number: 2013952640
ISBN: 978-0-06-232964-6
Printed in China, 2014

Illustration editing by Cam Floyd

Dedicated to Lisa Nguyen, who should have been the exception

"He who pretends
to look on death
without fear,
lies."

— Jean-Jacques Rousseau, Julie, or the New Heloise

"We die only once
and
for such a long time."

—Molière

LOOK

It's an introduction

Oh hello, I'm not sure if we have met before. I'm Ken Tanaka. How are you? I am fine. Thank you very much. I'm glad to know that you are reading my picture book. It is my hope that the many happy animals and people in this book will help you understand the inevitable fate that awaits us all. Sometimes people ask me why I wrote a "children's book for grown-ups." People seem to think that children need to be sheltered from the idea of death, but most children I have met are not afraid of death, or of this book. It is the grown-ups who shake in fear when they read the words Everybody Dies. Grown-ups are afraid of death. Grown-ups know that it is coming, and it can't be stopped.

When we are truly overcome with fear, we are still children on the inside, no matter our age. We still want our mommies. Sometimes grown-ups need to be treated like children for their own good. And so here it is, "Everybody Dies: A Children's Book for Grown-ups."

Although meant for adults, this book may be most effective when read aloud to frightened parents by their children.

Ken Tanaka

CUTE
ANIMALS DIE

AND SO DO SCARY ONES.

WHEN

GOLDFISH

DIE

THEY FLOAT TO THE

TOP OF THE TANK.

HONEY
BEES
DIE

Some Animals Live for a Very Long Time.

Mandrill
48 Years

Catfish
70 Years

Olm
Cave
Salamander
70 years

Giant
Tortoise
150
years

Geoduck
146 Years

Others Die Right Away.

NEITHER WILL MOMMY AND DADDY.

SOME PEOPLE TRY TO AVOID DEATH,

OTHERS TRY TO TEMPT IT,

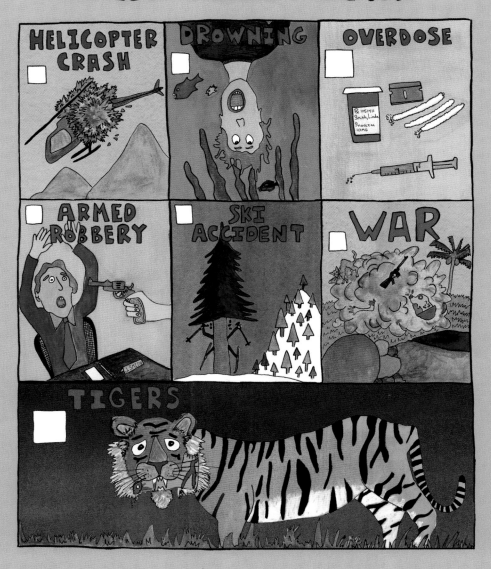

NO BODY LIKES TO THINK ABOUT DEATH,

BUT THE WORLD WOULD BE AWFULLY CROWDED WITHOUT IT.

Match the Corpse to the Cause of Death

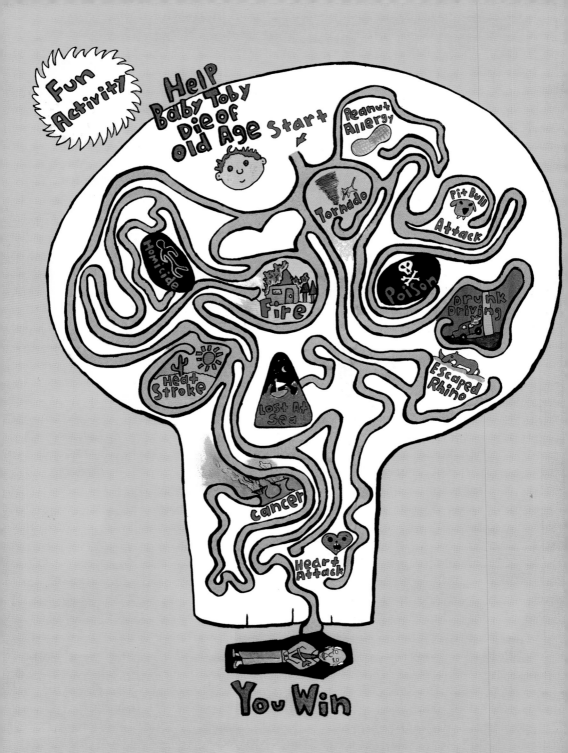

Exciting Careers in the Field of Death

Check out These

For More Information See Your Guidance Counselor

BUT YOU WON'T ALWAYS BE.

HERE ARE SOME DISEASES THAT COULD BE KILLING YOU RIGHT NOW

EVERYBODY DIES,

Fill out your very own Will*

Last Will And Testament
of _____

I _____, age _____, residing at _____ in
NAME
_____, being of sound mind, hereby declare
this to be my Last Will and Testament, revoking
all wills and codicils previously made by me.

1. I appoint _____ as my executor to
administer my estate. If _____ is unable or
unwilling to serve as my executor, then I
appoint _____ as my executor, and ask that
he/she be permitted to serve without court supervision
and to act without posting bond.

2. I hereby direct my executor to pay out all
legally enforceable claims against my estate and to
pay all federal and state inheritance taxes, administration
costs, expenses of my last illness and all funerary costs
without the intervention of the court.

3. I hereby bequeath my _____
_____ to _____
I hereby bequeath my _____
_____ to _____
I hereby bequeath my _____
_____ to _____

4. I hereby bequeath the remainder of my residuary estate to the following beneficiaries.

1. ____ % to _____

2. ____ % to _____

3. ____ % to _____

5. If any beneficiary listed above dies within thirty days of my own death, the deceased beneficiary's share shall be divided equally among the beneficiary's surviving children.

Self-Proving Affidavit

We the testator and the witnesses whose names are signed below do hereby declare that this instrument, consisting of these two pages, was the testator's Last Will and Testament, and that the testator, a legal adult appearing to be of sound mind, signed this instrument willingly, as a voluntary act, and was not under duress at the time of signing. Each witness hereby declares that the testator is not a minor. Each witness also declares that he/she signed this instrument at the request of and in the presence of the testator. We the witnesses each declare that each of us is over the age of eighteen and that each of us is and the other appears to be of sound mind. We each declare, under penalty of perjury, that the foregoing is true and correct and that this attestation and declaration are executed on the ____ day of ____ ____ at ____ (time).

Name _____   Address _____

Name _____   Address _____

THE
END

KEN TANAKA
PICTURE BOOKS
COLLECT THEM
ALL*

*(BOOKS do not actually exist)

KEN TANAKA LOVES YOU.

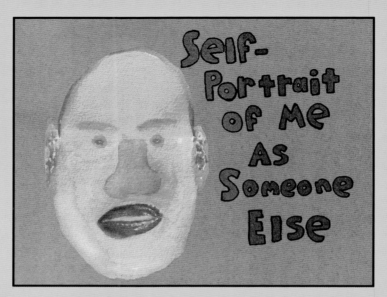

Self-Portrait of Me As Someone Else

Ken Tanaka

Born in Los Angeles as Ken Smith, Ken Tanaka was adopted by a Japanese family and raised in rural Shimane Prefecture. At the age of thirty-three, Ken returned to Los Angeles to search for his birth parents with only their names, Jonathan and Linda Smith. He documented his search on YouTube and quickly became an online sensation. His award-winning videos include the viral hit "What Kind of Asian Are You?", the White Samurai series, and "What Is Art?" In late 2007 Ken was reunited with his long-lost twin brother and "Everybody Dies" coauthor, David Ury, via YouTube (search Ken Tanaka meets David Ury on YouTube). The two of them have been collaborating ever since. When Ken is not busy with his search for the Smiths, he spends his time painting funny people and animals. In 2009 the famed Los Angeles gallery Billy Shire Fine Arts held his now-historic inaugural art show, "Maximum Pleasant," a humorous blend of Japanese and American pop culture. You can visit his art and animal friends at WWW.KenTanakaLovesYou.Com.

David Ury

Author, actor, and stand-up comic David Ury has a long history with death. While he is best known for getting crushed by an ATM as the character Spooge in AMC's "Breaking Bad", he has been shot, bitten, impaled, and stabbed to death countless times in American films and television programs. David's first acting role was in a high school production of "Riders to the Sea." He played the role of Bartley, an Irish fisherman who spent most of the play lying dead onstage, which made his mother cry. He has written nearly one hundred English language adaptations of foreign comics including "Me and the Devil Blues", which won a Glyph Award in 2009. You can find his work at WWW.DavidUry.Com.

Thank You

This book would not have been possible without the support of the following very handsome friends and animals.

Mari, Hideo and Junpei Tanaka, Jonathan and Linda Smith, Leah and Naomi, James Jean, Karen and Carl, Frank and Debra, Gary Musgrave, Signe Bergstrom, Keith Knight, Lonnie Millsap, Jacob the happy rabbit, Todd Moyer, Cam Floyd, SkU, Stella Choe, Naomi Grossman, Pay Katsuyuki, Dolly, Paul, and Carrie, David Mack, Josh Glaser, Billy Shire, Lucas Gray, Lebasse Projects, Mari Araki, Julia Abramoff, Deanne Oi, Takeo-Kun, Polo-Kun, Jerry Leibowtz, Jordan Feldman, Ria Fay-Berquist, Matt Murdock, Annie Adjchavanich, Remi February, Kitsune Suzuki, YouTube, Ginmeabreakman, Hikosaemon, You (The one reading this right now) Everyone at D.H. and Armada, Jordan Smith, Miles Beller

And our Sponsor

Daizen brand Mineral Water

TANAKA

The Wettest Water in the World